Into the Blue

by Maria d. Duarte Ortiz

Copyright © 2025 Kelp Books LLC

All rights reserved.

The characters and events portrayed in this book
are fictitious. Any similarity to real persons,
living or dead is coincidental and not intended.

No part of this book may be reproduced,
or stored in a retrieval system or transmitted
in any form or by other means, electronic,
mechanical, photocopying, recording
or otherwise without express written
permission of the publisher.

ISBN-13: 978-1-964880-07-5

Cover design and Illustrations: Leslie Gonzalez

Printed in the United State of America

TABLE OF CONTENTS

I.

Listen

In Nature

Dawn of Solitude

Spring Rain

Broken Clock

Consumer

I Got Lost in the Cascade

Frozen

6:29 p.m.

II.

The Night

Yearning for Home

Promises

Theory of Love

6:15 p.m.

In the Light of the Night

Absence

Falling in _____

Memories (remembrance)

In a Sunny Day

Writing You on the Page

Tell Me What To Do in a Starry Night

III.

A choice

The art of being broken

When dying

A drought

Living

Detoxicating love

Ripped Lips

At the end of the day, I drink

Heartbroken

1:38 p.m.

Limbo as a Dreamer

3:39 p.m.

The Monster

IV.

That weekend

Sleepless

This Letter

In the mirror burning

4:29 p.m.

The art of letting go

My humanity

12:56 p.m.

I am alone

4:09 p.m.

Dreams

I.

Listen

to the sound of silence
over open waters
hovering by this tiny
boat marking its way
to   the   end   of   the   horizon

In Nature

we are infinites
atoms circling in our blood
stretching our skin
frizzing our hair
opening our eyes and ears
to the end of the horizon

Dawn of Solitude

I dance in
all directions
a combination of
Salsa and Bachata
it feels like
I have no bones
no muscles
no nerves
only energy
dissolving
in the air
becoming
bits of lights

Spring Rain

falling
     just
          falling

it
 weeps
     in my heart

greening branches

     day
  turns to dusk
stops
    in a flower bed

Broken Clock

The morning is chill,
the birds fly away from their nest,
the sun woke up at 5:47am today,
dads get out of the door by 8am,
moms wake up with the little ones
to take them to school at 8:15am,
I drink coffee at 9:13am
and the rain stops by for a bit at 11:11am
the office goes to lunch at 12pm,
the mailman walks into the building at 1:45pm
at 2pm everything stops
I go to work,
at 3pm the clientele is low,
another coffee break at 3:47pm
at 4pm someone walks into the restaurant
at 5pm I go to lunch
everything stops again at 7:47pm when
I start my car to head home but instead
at 8:10pm I am drinking an old fashioned
at 9:37pm is time to go home,
did I live at all today?

Consumer

I.

And into the night I go sleepwalking
like a zombie, dreaming of the lace dress
I want to buy from Gilt.com
Is this a tragedy? Because it doesn't look
like a comedy or even a romance. The only
light comes from the computer screen ready
to jump to life in this darkness and dress itself
like Edward Scissorhands to cut me off
from this addiction of seeing but not buying.
My fingers ache with every stroke,
with every click because even though the items
are in the basket that basket will never be checked out.

II.

The night grows deep; my lips are dry
and my eyes are not as accurate as earlier.
What has become of me?
The malady of wanting every thing and not
having a single penny to own one item.
If I could afford one, I think I would be happy.
I think I would be less bitchy about those
who have more than I do, those who do not
work as hard as I do and have everything
but then are those people happy?
Are the items they ware their happiness?
And why do we need to own more than three
pairs of pants and shoes and skirts and shirts
and dresses? Are we masking our unhappiness
with bright colors?

III.

The night almost ends and I am still clicking
those keys searching for that perfect dress which
will make my tummy stand less, wanting that $300
dollar purse, thinking that another swimsuit will
suit me better than the one I have. But am I also
looking for a better face? One that could hide
the miserable state of my bones, one that would
be younger and less grouchy about life?

I Got Lost in the Cascade

of this empty city
I walk dead end streets
with purposeless steps

but I do not look up
and the sunrise comes
like a slow wave
unable to stop

Frozen

The air is still, and I can see my hands move
through the atoms of my pocket like water.

My pulse rests on the edge
of the table where my hands stand.

The heat of the sun comes at 5:47am.
My stomach rumbles, hot coffee dissipates
but I cannot feel you in the arteries of my heart.

6:29 p.m.

Your
breath
is still
on the
tulip
between
my breasts

II.

The Night

the rain stopped
while the wind continued

I had stopped
while you continued

the night passed
slowly
slowly I began to kiss you
and could not stop

could not stop
from feeling your skin
your hands on my thighs
your breath on my breasts
your thrust
your eyes gazing
your calling for more

Yearning for Home

The distance between oceans
that space that mumbles
empty air, a suffocation
of hurricanes, the land of palm
trees, and sweaty armpits,
a humid desire to fan yourself
with anything structurally sound,
the hills turning into ocean,
time stuck on bags of sliced mango
splatter with salt, lemon and
Valentina and the sun never
letting you forget the faces
of your grandparents sitting
on the porch of the ranch
watching the curtain of mist
cover the land of coffee

Promises

I can give you the heart of the flames
burning the chunks of my body.
I can give you the flames of the shooting
star crossing the scarlet sky.
I can give you the star in the center
of the rose raising at dawn.
I can give you the rose inside a chocolate box.
I can only give you a chocolate bar.

Theory of Love

And how does it feel to wake up with you by my side?
How do you take your coffee? Milk? Cream? Sugar?
And your eggs and bacon? Do you even like them?

How long it takes to grow a rose in my garden?
Or how many light years would take me to get to
Pluto? Or how slow the snail slides from point A to B?

Or do I know how it feels to kiss your lips without
thinking of her lips? Or make love to you wondering
if she does it better than I do? And do you like to bite
her nipples as you do to mine? And do you like to see
her naked too? Because she is beautiful.

But what really propelled you to come to me?
Dissatisfaction? Adventure? Routine?
All of the above and what is love?
What really is love? It's consistency?
It's ratio? It's dimensions? It's formula?
The components? The atoms?

Is there any question to get the result I want?
If life were as math I would not be in this theory
of finding out how it feels to be the other woman.

6:15 p.m.

And the light dies
inside the crevices left
by bubbles of saliva
of your kisses.

The sun rests on the horizon
sounds dissipate on the walls
of this coffee shop
and the image of myself
disappears in the mirror.

In the Light of the Night

The house is cold
air has come to chill my skin
the rays of the sun appear
underneath the palm trees
your arms are around me
unaware of the tears on my cheeks
of the silence whispering in my heart
of the pain your love is causing
this foreign feeling
I am afraid

Absence

The distance between us comes to me as a bull enraged;
all that anger directed towards my gut.

I have cried for a month without noticing the light
on my window, darkness crept in my heart, and I could
not stop crying trying to understand this business of loving.

I do not want to be part of this,
watching hummingbirds suck honey from flowers,
roaming the world, a temporary empty shell.

Falling in _____

The end came
before
the beginning
like lighting.

I thought
it was permanent
but permanence
is fleeting.

The sun comes
through my window
every morning
I cry because
the moon is gone.

Memories (remembrance)

I have images of kissing you your lips
their contour their ridges I can taste them
I can savor them your flesh
and yet what it hurts the most is the memory
I miss your warmth I am cold every night
my heart feels full, but I have nothing
only the blue of the night when I am able
to lose myself in everyone else's words
but I want my own words   I want my own
expressions I do not like repetition
and yet I feel I am saying everything that
has been said my soul is blue blue is sanity
a movie I play back every night of my day
would amnesia be better than to remember
every step taken?

In a Sunny Day

I am only left
with my silence

it was impossible
to make you love me

Writing You on the Page

I have to take you out
of my blood
the smell of your
cologne still lingers
in the pores of my skin
your smile still
resonates in the retina
of my eyes
I can still remember
the flavor of your saliva
my heart bleeds
through the tears
there is evidence
of our love making
under my nails

Tell Me To Do Without You in a Starry Night

Stare
at the
sky
and
cry

III.

A choice

A loaded gun doesn't
work for me.
Who will pull the trigger?
Who will be the one to have
that frozen moment in their
mind forever?

The art of being broken

My body has not survived this stillness,
this wanting to strip my skin and resurrect
the one I do not talk about.
This parting bleeds not as I want it,
not as a unity,
but as a smudge desiring to belong
and being unable to.
I have become the oily part of the salad
dressing in this relationship. But then again,
what relationship?

When dying

It is not true what they say
it is not the light you see last

it is the crashing of the waves
parakeets singing
a rose expanding its petals
the distance between hearts

it is the silence in them
that you hear the most

A drought

The river of my body
has dried
today there is no more water
to share with somebody
I am no longer an oasis
but a desert that expands
as the years pass
one day my skin will disintegrate
into sand and crumble as
you touch me in the middle
of a starry night

Living

And there is darkness
an empty tunnel
which exits every two
blocks without a sign
of which exit to take

then there is a roller
coaster going 4003 miles
per hour.   I do not stop
to throw up or even catch
a glimpse of the city below

after I'm thrown into the grass
where the undulating light blinds
me   not knowing where to go
I close my eyes and feel my dull
body fall into the hole that never ends

Detoxicating Love

Your body has been gone for a month
the butterflies in my stomach are not dead
but my arteries have stopped giving my brain oxygen
your memory continues to carve space in the neurons
which make me cry every time I remember your face
or every time my body shivers because it wants you
next to me but I am a broken piano
my keys do not play the song that made my heart
jump of joy I cannot even put them together as a shaft
I don't care for ice cream as much as I did
spaghetti doesn't taste the same even though
the pasta is the same and the sauce I made
is from your recipe book
I stand alone with a broken guitar
with a fractured thought of who I was
but the moon keeps shinning

Ripped Lips

Give me the silence
of the creases on your lips
while the hummingbird
whispers the secrets
of the breeze by the ocean
where do I put the roses
meant for you
if the only thing left
for me is the pieces
of a broken heart

At the end of the day, I drink

I can feel the atoms of my body move
the little hairs of my legs become grass
dancing side to side erect like electricity

but this electricity is over when I see your eyes
because your gaze kills the enthusiasm of my lungs
to become exhausted or happy or alive

why does your electricity kills?
why does it become a lighting
hitting my chest and suddenly
I am born again
what kind of murderer are you?

Heartbroken

my limbs hang
like chains
with no purpose
with no resolution
waiting for the stillness
of the night

1:38 p.m.

The rain has stopped
only the evidence of a crying
sky remains stuck on windowpanes
those drops don't stay but slide
until there are no more
if I become one of them
would I disappear too?

Limbo as a Dreamer

I am floating in between
Dante's Inferno
and a field of marigolds
unable to distinguish
between the end and
my imagined ending

the smell of coffee
brings me
back to this night
where the obscurity
of the moon frightens me
for no shadow can appear
and the stillness of the night
shows me the faces of those
long gone

3:39 p.m.

Crazy
for feeling your hands on my stomach
for smelling your cologne on my skin
for wanting to go back
for wanting to kiss you
for wanting to bite you

the still air – a cold that penetrates
the layers of my skin next to yours

crazy
for thinking of you when I shouldn't
for wanting you here next to me

the tress dancing slowly to the wind
know what follows

my lips against your skin
the weight of your body on my chest

my heart beat   the still hours
the whisperings

I miss
your stubborn movements
bringing me nearer you

The Monster

Inside I am all powerful
I move things with my mind
and create worlds with my mouth
I bring darkness into the kitchen
while snapping my fingers
there are no boundaries
I am an all-around magician
one of the best if not the best

you hate me because you are my puppet
and can make you say things
you did not intend
tomorrow I will destroy you
with my words
I come when you least expect it
when you hate me
and when you love me

I am the child you will never have
I am the half you detest
I am the other part of you
that hides in the ark of darkness
and appears when it rains
when the coffee is recently made
when the moon calls
when the words dance on the page

IV.

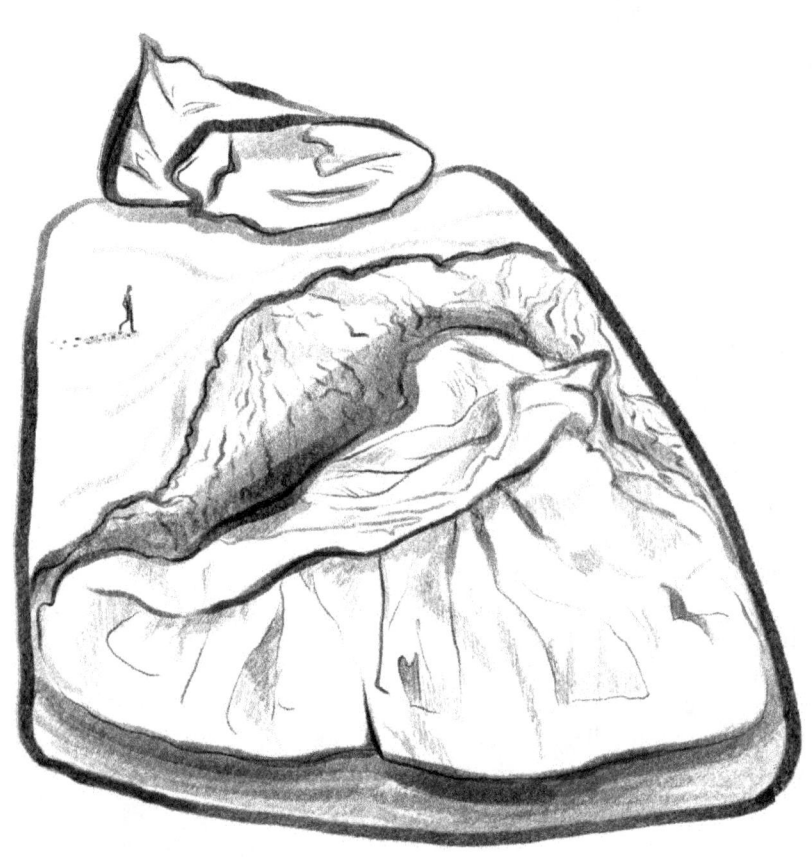

That weekend

It will never happen again
the desire to see you
the anxious look on the window
the humidity
the same sun but different feeling
the waiting for baggage
the excitement of catching a glimpse of you
the hug
your perfume
your smile
your eyes looking at me
your smile
you driving
me listening
me talking
me in silence
the room
the gifts
the holding hands
the watching the sunset
the kissing
the making love
the drinking
the partying
the talking
the making love
the eating
the drinking
the eating
the running for the bus
the rushed kiss
the letting go
the end

Sleepless

I have left the sheets of my bed
the skirt of the mattress is now untouched
while the lamp of my desk illuminates
the words scattered on the floor

there is no end to the space between you and me
even though I can touch you in my dreams
and it feels like failure this inability to forget
the ocean in my ear like a lullaby and your

body next to me asking for more of my boiling
skin to the point of exhaustion

This Letter

Dear,
     I don't have you near me tonight
I won't have you near me any time soon
I still remember your face and your smile
the dimples on your cheeks and your brown
eyes looking at me with an amazement
that amazed me   the tears roll down the piece
of skin you kissed so many times but now
they are dry waterfalls because I ran out of them
I do not smile anymore and the sadness in my eyes
has come back but that doesn't worry me I knew
that would happen   what I want is your skin
touching mine at night when it is too hot to sleep
I want your hands connecting with my nerves
making me shiver as if I was cold   I want you
as the essence of the hurricane that lives inside me

In the mirror burning

The cracking of my hair
the creases of my skin
melting
atom by atom
second by second
unable to stop
the patterns of myself
the movements of my hands
the gaze of my eyes
exhaling   inhaling
loving and hating the rest
of my mannequin self

4:29 p.m.

The distance between
my fingers is greater
than the distance between
my body and yours

the night howls
the air remains still
the act of leaving
is gathered with tequila
the act of vulnerability
is spread through the
wrestling of leaves
flying away in this
monotonous place

I gave you me
in a blurred state
not complete

The art of letting go

it is not based in any book
or technique passed
from generation to generation
it is about opening
the fingers one by one
feeling the ballon's string
come to an end

My humanity

Hollow trees are spared
from my memory while rain
taps on the incomplete windowsill

my skin absorbs light
through the glass –
I can see a rainbow

the end comes suddenly –
the hammer thundered
through the skies

do people become people for different reasons?

the leaves are the missing part
of this puzzle – the crushed bones
grow on fields of marigolds

looking at the display of summer
tearing soft pieces of land
through the concrete of ideas

the walnuts did not make it
the flies made them rot

sweet peas turned blue
lifting their heads upright
they flicker
before giving up their skeletons
to the wind

flames spared my eyes of footprints
left by calciferous bodies

clouds burst in exuberant colors
painting the sky not blue but multicolor

did the marigolds die too
in the fields of crushed bones?

12:56 p.m.

Thunder strikes
the quiet ocean
of clouds
lighting gives me
transparency

my other self covers
her eyes frighten
by the strength
of my voice

but the truth is
that I hide
behind her when
the light dies

I am alone

20 hours a day and
this is not a sad poem

I do not like snakes
or people who think
they are all that

I love love tulips
I think I am obsessed with them

there is a nest of birds
outside my window and
they chirp and chirp

and chirp without stopping
but this poem is not about birds

or the fact that I am alone
or about the tulips sitting on
the dining table

It is about discovering
another self that cannot
stay quiet

4:09 p.m.

The Chai latte on my chair
grows cold with the air of the fan

the days grow old as my eyes
smirk a little smile –

a little smile
I am not unhappy
yet –

the wind bothers me
my teeth grind with the moon
yet –

today
I lost my faith
my mother gave me

today
I became my own hope

Dreams

My mind is full of stored dreams,
they are stuck inside drinking a latte
in the imagined café and watching
a lecture on how to be free.

But none of these dreams matter as much
as the ones that have left, the ones flying
overhead where the sun is never down
and the horizon doesn't end.

They do not need praise or memorandums
they do not need ties to this old anchor
where rust eats the last chances to walk free;
they do not even need to be remembered
because they live.

ABOUT THE AUTHOR

Maria d. Duarte Ortiz received her MFA in Creative Writing from the University of California, Riverside – Palm Desert. She has published poems in *Verdad Magazine* and *The Good Grief Journal: A Journey Toward Healing*, in the anthology Here to Stay: Poetry and Prose from the Undocumented Diaspora, Los Angeles Poetry Beach 2022 and Kelp Journal. Her personal essay "Dear America" appears in Alta Journal and her Op-ed "As a 'Dreamer,' I'm never not afraid" appeared in the LA Times. She is currently the poetry editor for Kelp Journal and a CLI Alumna.

www.ingramcontent.com/pod-product-compliance
Lightning Source LLC
Chambersburg PA
CBHW062123080426
42734CB00012B/2970